Original title:
Life's Meaning: I Think It's in the Freezer

Copyright © 2025 Creative Arts Management OÜ
All rights reserved.

Author: Olivia Sterling
ISBN HARDBACK: 978-1-80566-260-0
ISBN PAPERBACK: 978-1-80566-555-7

Winter's Quiet Revelation

In the chilly depths, secrets hide,
Frozen delights, where dreams reside.
A box of treasures, meals on a shelf,
Even old soup feels just like itself.

I ponder my choices, within frosty walls,
Veggies and ice cubes hear my calls.
Do I want that last slice of cake?
Or a healthy salad? Oh, what a mistake!

The Icebound Journey of Thought

Adventures await in icy terrain,
Where leftovers linger, and thoughts remain.
Oh, jolly old pizza, you never grow stale,
On this frozen trip, I'm destined to sail.

With a swipe of the door, chills rush my face,
Eggnog from Christmas, oh, what a disgrace!
A fortress of flavor, it's hard to resist,
Lost in the ice, where nothing's amiss.

The Still Waters Beneath the Ice

Underneath the frost, a world of cheer,
Beneath the surface, it's delightfully clear.
Carrots frozen in lengthy repose,
Wait for a thaw, when comedy grows.

In the silence of chill, giggles emerge,
As frozen concoctions begin to surge.
What is the meaning, we laugh and we jest,
In a frosty realm, we find our best!

Unfrozen Laughter Echoes Millennia

In the freezer's embrace, we share a grin,
With icecream dreams, let the giggles begin.
Old pot pie tales and coleslaw's delight,
Unfrozen humor dances at night.

So gather your friends, let's raise a toast,
To all those snacks we love the most.
In the chill of the night, we find our zest,
In frozen moments, we're truly blessed.

Freezing Time in a World of Heat

In a kitchen where chaos reigns,
I open the door, laughter remains,
Frozen peas and ice cream dreams,
Time stands still, or so it seems.

An ice cube slips, a dance ensues,
My socks get wet, what a ruse!
Thawing out my grin, I see,
Life's just a chill, wild and free.

The frosty air, a breath of cheer,
I ponder joys that linger here,
A popsicle heart in summer's blaze,
Reminds me of those frosty days.

The Frosted Glass of Perception

Through the glass, the world looks bright,
I squint and laugh at the silly sight,
A frozen sandwich, a clever play,
Perception changes every day.

I sip my drink, it clinks with glee,
An iceberg floats through thoughts of me,
What's clear is often not so true,
Like ice cream melting, I'm confused too.

In frosty frames, we twist and shout,
Finding wisdom in things we doubt,
So grab a scoop, don't let it slide,
Chill out, my friend, let's enjoy the ride.

Icy Paths to Warm Souls

On frosty paths, I wander slow,
Slipping here, and there I go,
With each stumble comes a grin,
Finding warmth in laughter's spin.

Snowflakes land upon my nose,
I dance like no one really knows,
In chilly air, our hearts ignite,
A warmth surrounds in pure delight.

Ice cream cones in winter's blast,
Remind us that good times can last,
With each frozen step, we won't freeze,
Icy laughs and hearts at ease.

Layers of Ice and Echoes

Beneath the frost, there lies a tale,
Echoes of laughter, a joyful trail,
Like frozen layers of cake we slice,
Each bite reveals a little spice.

I stack my troubles, one by one,
Till they melt in sun, oh what fun!
Life's a buffet, a frosty feast,
Where joys abound and worries cease.

In winter's grip, let's not be shy,
We'll make snow angels in the sky,
With layers of ice beneath our feet,
We'll find our way, make it complete.

Savoring the Moments That Chill

In the corners, cool and bright,
Ice cream dreams take their flight.
Frozen peas and pints galore,
Memories wedged behind the door.

Each scoop whispers tales we keep,
Of laughter shared, and late night leap.
The chill captures our fleeting days,
In frosty wraps, where joy displays.

Echoes from a Frosted Past

I open wide the frosty door,
And find old pizza on the floor.
The memories cling, they dance around,
In layers thick, they can be found.

Frozen dinners, a time of haste,
In every bite, I can taste the waste.
Yet here I stand, with laughter bright,
Culinary ghosts in the moonlight.

The Unthawed Complexity of Being

A block of ice reveals the quirks,
Of fragile joys and playful quirks.
From veggies lost to ancient frost,
To things we savored, that we lost.

Unlocking things we left behind,
Odd souvenirs of the mind.
Each thaw a chance to reminisce,
In frosted shelves, we find our bliss.

Melting Memories of Yesterday

The sun peeks in, the ice cream slides,
As memories melt, and joy abides.
A drip or two brings back the cheer,
The heart rejoices, the laugh sincere.

In every scoop, the past takes flight,
With sprinkles of joy, a happy bite.
Oh, the sweetness in a simple treat,
In frozen moments, we feel complete.

Melting Memories into Tomorrow

In the frost, I hide my dreams,
Popsicles whisper silly schemes.
Lost socks dance in icy glee,
Laughter trapped like a frozen sea.

Each bite a giggle, each scoop a cheer,
Banana bread chilling, have no fear!
Frosted cupcakes, oh what a sight,
Memories melting, tasty delight.

The Chill of Reflection's Embrace

I opened the door, what a surprise!
Frozen pizza with two small eyes.
Leftovers lingering, a time machine,
A taco's tale, if only it could speak.

A block of ice, my thoughts unwind,
Each frosty layer, treasures I find.
Reflections giggle, as veggies freeze,
What a way to pause, with such ease!

Frosty Paths Yet to Wander

A frosty path of treats awaits,
Minty wonders and chocolate gates.
I strut with confidence, no need to rush,
Scooping joy, in a frosty hush.

Ice cubes jingle, a merry song,
In this chilly world, I belong.
With every crunch, the laughter flows,
Frozen whimsies, life's comedic shows.

The Shimmering Iceberg of Possibility

An iceberg full of dreams untold,
Jelly beans glimmer, daring and bold.
In the frosty depths, sweet hopes reside,
Chillin' like penguins, let's take a ride!

Whipped cream clouds and sprinkles galore,
A frosty treasure, who could want more?
Giggles in the freezer, what a delight,
With every cold bite, the future feels bright!

Frosted Dreams in Every Nook

In the cold, where hopes reside,
Leftover dreams, they try to hide.
Tucked behind a box of peas,
Lies a wish for summer breeze.

Milk jugs whisper stories true,
Of frozen moments, me and you.
Ice cubes dance in chilled delight,
Turning midnight into light.

The Icebox of Forgotten Wishes

Behind the door, a treasure trove,
Of birthday cakes and pop-tart love.
Condiments in lonely rows,
Waiting for a feast to pose.

Pickles dream of pickle brine,
On shelf where hopes and snacks entwine.
Hot dogs sigh beneath the chill,
Yearning for a grill, a thrill.

Chilled Echoes of Existence

A frosty laugh escapes the fridge,
Where frozen pizzas dream of kids.
Soft serve thoughts swirl in a cone,
In the twilight, chills are sown.

Ice cream sundaes tell their tales,
Of summer nights and wind in sails.
Leftover frowns that turn to glee,
Sweet reminders of jubilee.

Frosty Reflections on the Soul

Mirrors made of glassy frost,
Hiding dreams we thought we lost.
Chips and dips in cool embrace,
Fleeting moments time can't chase.

Wait for snacks, they call my name,
In this cool, there's no shame.
Frosted bites of joy and jest,
In this box, we find our rest.

When Time Stood Still in Cold

In the freezer, I sit a while,
Surrounded by pizzas, ice cream, and smile.
Time's frozen here, my worries too,
Like veggies that forgot to bid adieu.

The clock ticks slowly, but not a sound,
Among the frost, my thoughts abound.
A carrot waves like a queen so bold,
In this world where it's always cold.

The Hidden Treasures Beneath Ice

Buried beneath layers of frost,
Lies a stash, but at what cost?
Forgotten dinners from last July,
Their stories lost, they silently cry.

There's mystery in each frozen crisper,
Lost lunches that once held a whisper.
A tupperware time capsule of old,
Reheating the past, or so I'm told.

Glacial Moments of Clarity

In this chilly realm, ideas glide,
Thoughts flow easily, they never hide.
While popsicles dance in a frosty haze,
I ponder life through a frozen maze.

An ice cube's wisdom, so pure, so bright,
Teaches me patience in cold, quiet night.
As I sip my drink, the ice softly clinks,
In each crystal, a truth that thinks.

Icy Imprints of the Past

Last week's leftovers, an iceberg's tale,
Whispers of meals that once set sail.
Each container, a memory packed tight,
Frosted keepsakes that fade out of sight.

I see my youth in a frozen cake,
Joyful gatherings, not a mistake.
With each thaw, a story revived,
Among the ice, the past is alive.

Reflections in the Chilled Mirror

In the frozen depths, I spy,
Frosty faces passing by.
Ice cream smiles, a frosty cheer,
Who knew snacks would hold me dear?

In this cold, I find some peace,
Laughter wraps like a warm fleece.
Frozen dinners stacked so high,
As I ask the pizza pie.

Life feels sweet, if not a bit,
In this chill, I love to sit.
Veggies dance in frosty glee,
What's the rush? Just wait and see!

So let the world outside just spin,
With each scoop, I feel the win.
Frozen treasures, joy and glee,
In this box, I'm truly free.

Echoes of an Icy Heart

Whispers bounce off frozen walls,
Chilled confessions, laughter calls.
The frosty air greets me with a wink,
Skimpy sweaters? I don't think!

In ice cubes, secrets hide,
Bits of my chaos, what a ride!
Leftovers talk in muffled tones,
Sharing dreams of tasty bones.

With each trip to the icy shelf,
I ponder on my frozen self.
A block of ice, with humor sweet,
Where jokes and laughter have a seat.

So let them judge my frosty stash,
For in this chill, I've found my bash.
An echo of joy, a chilly start,
The humor glows from my icy heart.

Silent Crystals in the Chill

In the freezer, silence reigns,
Crystal laughter, never wanes.
From frosty shelves, the jokes arise,
Yogurt giggles, oh what a surprise!

Frozen peas, they roll and sway,
In this chill, we'll laugh and play.
Snowy treats with tales to tell,
A frosty kingdom where I dwell.

The ice cream sings a creamy tune,
Under stars of a frozen moon.
Frigid delights, they sparkle bright,
In the stillness, joy takes flight.

So come and share this frosty song,
In this chill, you can't go wrong.
Amidst the quiet, laughs will spill,
As we savor life in the chill.

Frigid Whispers of Tomorrow

Tomorrow waits in icy peace,
Chilled delights that never cease.
Frosty dreams in boxes neat,
Hope and humor blend so sweet.

The frozen clock ticks slowly by,
With popsicles that seem to fly.
new flavors come, then quickly go,
What will stick? Oh, it's a show!

As frosty winds begin to howl,
I chuckle softly, life's a prowl.
Tomorrow's plans in frosted jars,
Chasing dreams beneath the stars.

So grab a scoop of fun today,
Let frozen joy lead the way.
In chilly corners, hope will grow,
Through frigid whispers, we'll just glow.

Chilling Tranquility of Stowed Time

In the depths where icebergs sleep,
Time takes on a frozen leap.
Leftovers laugh in frosty glee,
Whispering secrets just for me.

A pizza slice, a taco charm,
They huddle close, no cause for alarm.
While outside life can feel so loud,
In here, I'm cozy, wrapped in a shroud.

Once a banquet, now a frost,
Memories lost or perhaps just tossed.
With every thaw, a tale unfolds,
In chill and freeze, life's laughter holds.

So here I sit with my frosty feast,
Among frozen friends, I am at peace.
In this chilly cavern, fun abounds,
As time is stowed in frosted rounds.

Shimmering Secrets of the Freezer

Behind the door, where treasures gleam,
A frosty realm, a cold daydream.
Frozen pizzas, peas in a row,
Each holds a tale, a quirky show.

Ice cubes dance like a happy crew,
Chillin' hard with a frosty view.
The popsicles hum a jaunty tune,
While ice cream winks at the warm moon.

Leftovers have their own wild chat,
"Remember when? Oh, where was that?"
In each icy block, a laughter glows,
As secrets bubble beneath the snows.

So come explore this icy lore,
Where fun is found behind the door.
In frozen states, joy holds its ground,
In shimmering shapes, life's quirks abound.

The Subtle Taste of Icy Remembrance

In the frost, memories intertwine,
A hint of laughter, a splash of brine.
A half-eaten cake, a soup from last fall,
Each frosty bite brings back a call.

With every peek, the past replays,
In chilly bites, nostalgia stays.
Frozen moments, sweet and sour,
A gourmet feast of time's own power.

These icy pockets hold memories dear,
A pot roast party or Monday cheer.
In the cool embrace where time slips tight,
A frosty smile greets the night.

So let's unwrap the frozen past,
Taste the joy that was built to last.
In every bite, a story sings,
Of warmth and chill and funny things.

Frosty Hues in the Palette of Time

In hues of frost, the palette lays,
A cupboard filled with frosty plays.
Colorful veggies, stark and bright,
Each one tells of a chilly night.

Blueberry crumbles, a sweet delight,
All waiting for the right invite.
Time drips slowly in icy hues,
As laughter wafts in morning's muse.

Frosted jars of past delights,
Each brings laughter, each ignites.
The season's chill wraps around my heart,
Crafting art from icy parts.

So let us savor these frosty views,
A palette rich with colorful clues.
In frozen frames of time, we find,
A joyful feast for heart and mind.

Snow-Capped Hopes in the Dark

In the quiet hum of a chilling breeze,
Frozen dreams sway like idle trees.
When cravings strike and the heart does race,
Look to the cooler, that joyful space.

A frosty world where treasures lie,
Pizza slices, oh my, oh my!
Laughter bubbles with each frozen bite,
Who knew the fridge held such delight?

Hopes packed tight in tidy rows,
Mysteries linger where cold wind blows.
Kale and ice cream share a glance,
In this frosty wonder, we prance.

When the house feels barren, go take a look,
Past the veggies and that old recipe book.
For in the chill of a sparkling glow,
Your quirky joys may just overflow.

The Glimmer of Ice-Crowned Thoughts

Beneath layers of frost, there lies a spark,
Ideas dance in the chilly dark.
A lonely burrito waits with pride,
Craving humans to come inside.

Thoughts freeze quickly, like ice on a lake,
Yet laughter warms the choices we make.
Pickles slumber, their tang still bright,
Ready to serve on a whimsy night.

In this kingdom of cold, the colors shine,
Frosty delights, oh how divine!
From cravings born under neon lights,
A quirky feast of laughing bites.

Remove the frost with a gentle touch,
Rediscover joy that means so much.
In every shelf, a tale unfolds,
In the heart of the chill, humor never grows old.

Beneath the Surface of Stillness

There's a world below the chilly sheen,
Leftovers whisper with secrets unseen.
A cupcake hides, adorned with frost,
A past celebration, never lost.

In the realm of ice, creativity spins,
Yesterday's dinner, where adventure begins.
Grab a spoon, and dig in with glee,
Finding joy where it's meant to be.

Every container holds smiles in wait,
Like frozen laughter upon my plate.
The soup of wisdom, the stew of cheer,
Come partake, let's feast without fear.

Among the stillness, chaos does play,
In the cubic tundra, let's dance away.
A flick of the lid, let merriment rise,
In a world so cold, surprise is the prize.

A Symphony of Frozen Echoes

In the silence of frost, hear the echoes call,
A symphony brewing within four walls.
Frozen peas and a half-eaten pie,
Join together to laugh and sigh.

Frosty rhythms tap on the glass,
Ice cubes chime as the moments pass.
A churning laugh in the rhythm of chill,
When the fridge is a stage, you get your fill.

Beneath the lid, a concert awaits,
With flavors that play through the open gates.
Melodies rise with a bubbling cheer,
As friends gather 'round, the joy is near.

So lift your fork, let's sing along,
To the silly tunes of the food-filled throng.
In the symphony of frost and fun,
Together we dine, till the day is done.

Frigid Paths to Uncovered Dreams

In frosty realms of ice and cheer,
We seek the joys we hold so dear.
A nugget lost, a pint of grace,
Frozen treasures in their place.

With every scoop, a wish fulfilled,
A dash of hope, a heart instilled.
Lost in the frost, we find our way,
Dreams once cold now boldly play.

The Thawing of Hidden Histories

Behind the doors of winter's keep,
Lies tales of joy that make us leap.
Each container holds a story bright,
As flavors dance in pure delight.

From frozen peas to stale cake bites,
We thaw the past in quirky sights.
Resurrected meals, they wave and cheer,
What once was cold is now sincere.

A Colder Grasp on the Now

In icy grasp, we find our wit,
With jokes and gags, we never quit.
Chilled emotions take a spin,
We laugh aloud, let the fun begin!

A frosted pie, we take a slice,
Savoring moments, oh so nice.
Life unfreezes with each bold bite,
A humor found in chilly light.

Insight in a Frosted Frame

Behind the glass so frosty clear,
Lies wisdom wrapped in frozen cheer.
Each icy glance, a fleeting thought,
What's lost in cold, we once sought.

Reflecting back with a frosty grin,
In frozen frames, we all begin.
As warmth returns, so too do we,
To answer what was meant to be.

Reflections in a Frosted Pane

In the chill of a frosty view,
I ponder things I wish I knew.
Vegetables stare from their frozen tombs,
While leftovers plot their culinary dooms.

Are ice cream dreams truly sublime?
Or just whispers lost in the grind of time?
A stew of thoughts, simmering slow,
In a tundra where no sun can glow.

Perhaps frozen peas hold the grand truth?
Like deep secrets waiting for sleuths.
Yet, I find joy in this icy jest,
Who knew that the freezer could be so blessed?

As I chuckle at frosty delights,
I contemplate life on cold winter nights.
In chilly corners, laughter takes flight,
With humor wrapped in every bite.

Heartbeats in a Frigid Frame

With a blast of cold, the heart doth race,
In a chilly space, I find my place.
Frozen pizzas smile back at me,
While I ponder the tough facts of reality.

The frostbitten shelves tell tales of old,
Of dinners gone wrong and stories retold.
Yet, in this deep freeze, there's wisdom to find,
Like pizza that's perfect when the stars align.

A frosty realm where time takes a break,
And days blend together like an ice cream shake.
In each chilly nook, a heartbeat is cast,
Reminding me fun moments are meant to last.

So I laugh with the pint of mint chocolate chip,
A frosty adventure on a frosty trip.
For every beat, a giggle uncored,
In this winter's embrace, I find I'm adored.

Winter's Whisper in Every Corner

In the corners of frost, tales softly speak,
Of carrots and cakes, all at their peak.
Whispers of winter mingle and tease,
As I navigate through the cold with ease.

A frosty friend in the deep freeze lies,
With pickles and pizzas all covered in ice.
Yet within this gelid, expansive expanse,
I find a curious reason to dance.

A frosted silence reigns in the air,
As leftovers giggle, a sight quite rare.
In each frigid crack, laughter's not far,
Even while munching a well-cooked bazaar.

So here's to the chill and the things we save,
In winter's embrace, we're all quite brave.
From nuggets of fun to frozen surprises,
Life's hilarity grows with each cold disguise.

Preserved Moments in the Cold

In a world so brisk, moments freeze tight,
Captured within, they glimmer and bite.
The fruits of my labor sit still in time,
While ice crystals cradle a rhythm and rhyme.

Each shelf holds memories clutched in a chill,
Temptations await with a whim and a thrill.
From ice pops of summer to soups stowed away,
In the heart of the frost, we find our own play.

As I gaze through the frost at a colorful spread,
I giggle at veggies that once gave me dread.
They whisper sweet secrets of comfort and cheer,
Encased in the cold, they make mischief here.

With every scoop from this wintry delight,
I savor the moments that sparkle and bite.
So here's to the fun in the frozen nest,
Where laughter resides and life truly rests.

In the Depths of the Deep Freeze

In the cold depths of our fridge,
There lies more than just old bread.
A frozen laugh, a frosty smile,
Awaiting for fun, instead of dread.

Chilled leftovers of past delight,
Resting patiently, calm and bright.
Fridge magnets hold my memories,
Waving like sails in frozen night.

Mystery meals wrapped tight, oh yes,
Time travelers in icy dress.
They vibrate stories, loud and bold,
An epic feast, a frosty mess.

When life gets tough, I'll pop a tray,
Dance with peas in a silly way.
Each frozen morsel, a silly cheer,
Come, join the feast, what fun, I say!

Memories Preserved in Ice

In frosty tombs of glacial hue,
I stash my past, a chilly view.
With every cube of slushy zest,
Memories frozen, oh how they brew.

Old pizza slices laugh in glee,
A date with mustard? Oh, what a spree!
Stale cake, deserving of a crown,
Waving like flags, just wait and see.

Pull out the tub, and take a peek,
Banana bread, still looking chic.
Each bite a tale, each spoonful sings,
Of half-baked dreams, and days unique.

In ice we trust, we find our cheer,
A laugh, a hug, our friends draw near.
Frozen treasures tucked away tight,
In cold silence, their stories clear.

The Frosty Pause of Reflection

When life gets heavy, cold as snow,
I find a pause in the freezer's glow.
Take a breath, let time freeze still,
Humor grows when icy winds blow.

Frosty echoes giggle in my space,
Coffee from last week? A bold embrace!
I ponder jokes in frozen air,
Amid the veggies, life's playful chase.

A cold stew bubbling with lost laughs,
Frozen hopes tucked in plastic halves.
This chilly realm of silly sorrows,
Collects the cheer, the warmth that halves.

So here I sit, in chilled repose,
With every bite, a ticklish prose.
In icy corners, joy is found,
A quirky dance, how quickly it grows!

Frozen Feasts of the Spirit

In ice and frost, our spirits soar,
Fried chicken dreams from days of yore.
Lost in ice, they wait for cheer,
Craving laughter, let's explore!

A banquet of jests just waiting there,
A frozen feast with resolutions rare.
Together we dine, our hearts entwined,
In this cold sanctuary, our worries share.

With every scoop of creamy grin,
Potatoes frolic, how they spin!
Nostalgic bites bring laughter loud,
In chilly company, let the fun begin!

So grab a spoon, join in the jest,
This icy gathering, a lively quest.
In frosty feasts of spirit bright,
We'll savor smiles, it's for the best!

Frozen Whispers of Existence

In the chill of the fridge, dreams do reside,
Half-baked ideas, tucked away inside.
Whispers of ice cream, sweet and so cold,
Frosty ambitions, waiting to unfold.

Veggies in bags, oh what a sight,
Staring back at me every night.
Leftovers mingle, they all seem to say,
'We once had a purpose, now we're just gray!'

The freezer hums softly, like a lullaby,
Chilling my thoughts, making them fly.
Slippers and socks, tucked in so neat,
What's the meaning? More snacks to eat!

So I ponder while munching on a treat,
Is existence just frozen pizza for heat?
Laughter erupts as I open the door,
Perhaps the answers are way down on the floor!

Thawing the Heart of the Matter

Frosted emotions in a cold metal box,
Churning and swirling like baffled ox.
Searching for guidance in frozen delights,
Hope hides in ice cubes on cold winter nights.

Defrosting my heart, a daring endeavor,
Will I find warmth or regret forever?
A popsicle's dream of a sunlit shore,
Melting the woes that I can't ignore.

Pickles and memories, all in a jar,
Trading their stories, oh how bizarre!
Could mustard hold wisdom? I'm starting to think,
Perhaps it's the ketchup that'll help me not sink.

So I'll thaw out each thought, take my time,
Turning ice into fun – yes, that's the rhyme!
With spoons and laughter, I dig right in,
Finding the heart where ice used to win!

Ice-Cold Reflections

Staring inside, it's a glittery show,
Frozen reflections, oh where did they go?
Eggs look like stars in this glacial expanse,
While the milk dreams of a tropical dance.

Meatballs in winter wear, oh what a sight,
Gearing up for adventures, ready to fight!
Peas in their packets, all shaking in glee,
'What's the point?' they croak, 'Can't you see?'

Laughter echoes amidst chilled cuisine,
Frosty debates on what could have been.
Potatoes contemplating their fate by the day,
Thinking 'why not just bake us right away?'

So I ponder these thoughts, it's humor I find,
In a freezer of wonders, both silly and blind.
I'll scoop up my joy with a spoon and a grin,
Finding meaning in laughs; let the fun begin!

Chilling Thoughts in a Frigid World

In a land of ice cubes, frozen delight,
Thoughts skate around, a comical sight.
Broccoli's wisdom, oh what can it teach?
That greens are just here, not out of reach.

Discussions with butter, so creamy and sage,
'Chill out!' it laughs, 'Don't act like a cage!'
Sauces conspire in the deep frosty void,
Reminding me gently, I'm far from destroyed.

As I rummage through layers, a treasure hunt quest,
Searching for solace in what I love best.
From pizza to popsicles, all in a row,
Each bite a giggle, making joy overflow.

So let's dance through the frost, in laughter we'll glide,
Finding purpose in warmth where the coolness resides.
In the world of the frigid, I take a big leap,
Discovering humor in what's ours to keep!

Inspections in the Icebox of Time

In the chilly depths I delve,
Where frozen treasures quietly dwell.
Leftovers whisper tales of yore,
Cabbage from last fall, who could ask for more?

Frostbitten peas in a plastic bag,
Waving at me like a hungry flag.
A pizza from 2019, still intact,
I ponder its fate, do I take the act?

Lost hopes in ice, they slumber still,
Dreams of dinners that once had thrill.
I check the dates like a frigid sage,
Funny how time can freeze a page.

Yet in this cold, the laughter's bright,
A midnight snack brings sheer delight.
With every bite, I find a spark,
In my icebox, I ignite the dark.

The Cold Truth Beneath Every Layer

Under layers of foil, what do I find?
A gift from a friend, long left behind.
Is it soup or broth? A mystery deep,
In the world of chill, the secrets keep.

Frosty veggies, their colors bold,
Tales of harvest, if they only told.
A half-eaten cake from a birthday bash,
Begging for attention, but what a clash!

The cold truth stares back with a wink,
A tub of yogurt, its fate on the brink.
I laugh at the thought, this icy charade,
In every container, a quirky parade.

So here's to the artifacts, strange and rare,
Each frozen find makes me stop and stare.
With laughter and joy, I reach for a slice,
In this fridge of wonders, everything's nice!

Glimpse of the Past Through Frosted Glass

Peering through frost, I see my days,
Jars of pickles, in their merry haze.
A scoop of ice cream with a story to tell,
In this wonderland, all is well.

Leftover lasagna, a cheesy delight,
Waving hello in the pale moonlight.
Pick out the noodles, where did they roam?
Shall I take a trip, or leave them alone?

This chilly view is a comedy show,
A past life playing in frozen tableau.
Each layer reveals a different scene,
Nostalgia wrapped in foil, so serene.

As I venture deeper into the frost,
Each splat and spill, I wonder the cost.
In this glassy abode, laughter won't cease,
For every cold bite, I find my peace.

The Serenity of a Frozen Moment

In the freezer's grasp, there's a pause so sweet,
A time capsule of meals, a whimsical treat.
Chillin' like villains, those leftovers gleam,
In this icy world, they're the ultimate dream.

Egg rolls from last week, still holding their pride,
A saga of crunch, they simply can't hide.
Pints of ice cream tell tales of despair,
How I conquered a week with courage and flair.

A moment preserved, I chuckle aloud,
As I rummage through frost, oh, isn't it proud?
Every chunk and morsel a story unique,
Frozen in laughter, there's treasure to seek.

So here's to the freezer, my humorous friend,
Where memories linger, time seems to bend.
In every frozen pocket, a joy I can savor,
For in these cold depths, I find my favor.

In the Hush of the Chilling Air

In the hush of the chilling air,
Frozen peas make me stop and stare.
Life's secrets hid behind glass doors,
With every frost, my laughter soars.

Another pint of ice cream awaits,
It giggles softly, never berates.
Pickles and berries lined up in rows,
They all hold tales that nobody knows.

A half-eaten cake, a moment frozen,
Reminds me of parties we've chosen.
Mysterious frost on the window pane,
Whispers of joy wrapped up in grain.

So here I stand, with a spoon in hand,
In a world so cold, it's perfectly grand.
I've found my fortune, my treasure chest,
In the freezer's chill, I feel truly blessed.

Preserved Joys in Frigid Spaces

In frigid spaces, the laughter glows,
With every opening, the chill just flows.
Bags of frozen peas, the jester's delight,
Making meals festive, a frosty bite.

The remnants of dinner, all stored away,
They chuckle softly, waiting their day.
A lasagna that waves, 'Remember me?'
In this icy land, we live carefree.

Frosted cupcakes, just sitting so still,
Whispering secrets that give me a thrill.
Every treat tucked in with loving care,
In the frost, there's humor beyond compare.

So here's to the fun that the cold can bring,
In preserved joys, my heart starts to sing.
The enchantment of meals that I can't forget,
In icy chambers, I have no regret.

The Echoes of Cold Comfort

The echo is soft, in the coolness I find,
A chorus of snacks, all perfectly aligned.
Frozen treasures in a world that spins,
In every shelf, a giggle begins.

Muffins in wrappers, a frosted surprise,
They wink from their boxes, a dessert in disguise.
The fridge hums gently, a comforting tune,
As I search for gems beneath the full moon.

A banquet of ice, where veggies convene,
In their chilly embrace, nothing's too mean.
Onions and peppers in a frost-tipped dance,
Caught in the freeze, they twirl and prance.

So here's to the joy that's tucked away tight,
In the echoes of cold, I find pure delight.
With every new frostbite, I chuckle and cheer,
In this chilly world, comfort's always near.

Whispers of Ice in a Warm World

In a warm world, whispers softly call,
From icy chambers, they beckon us all.
Frozen delights in a frosty embrace,
With a wink from the shards, I find my place.

Mysterious bundles in frosty attire,
Flavors and fables beneath layers of fire.
Each bite that I take is a giggle revealed,
In the chill of the night, joy is concealed.

The laughter of ice, a delightful refrain,
In a sea of warmth, it's never mundane.
With cupcakes and sorbet, my heart takes flight,
In this blend of nature, I savor the night.

As shadows grow long, my humor is bright,
With whispers of ice, I embrace the night.
In these frozen moments, I find my bliss,
With a smile and a snack, I can't help but wish.

Cold Comforts Underneath the Layers

In the chill of the fridge, I find my peace,
Leftover dreams waiting for release.
A squishy carrot, a half-formed pie,
Calls for a feast as I sigh and cry.

Frozen treasures whisper tales untold,
Of bad dinners missed and adventures bold.
Each layer a story, stacked up just right,
I dive into flavors that dance in the night.

Ice cubes clinking, a symphony sweet,
While broccoli lurks with a flaccid defeat.
I rummage through packages, student delights,
Dinner plans canceled on long phone nights.

Yet amidst these cold comforts, I do not complain,
A citrusy surprise might just wane the pain.
With each bite I take, with each laugh I share,
I'm frozen in time, but without a care.

An Icy Sanctuary of Past Lives

In the depths of the freezer, a time capsule waits,
Old pizza slices hold mysterious fates,
Potato skins whisper of parties gone by,
While ice cream remembers the day I did cry.

Popsicles hide, aging gracefully slow,
Once vibrant in color, now statues of woe.
A mangled cucumber, all shriveled and gray,
Still somehow tells stories of better days play.

Yearning for laughter, and a bite gone wrong,
I search through the frosty and sing my song.
A fridge door creaks like an old wooden boat,
Sorting through memories, flavors in coat.

Tucked in the corner, a dinner disaster,
Reminds me of making great haste, not much faster.
Yet when I unearth all these treasures so cold,
Laughter and warmth, in my heart they fold.

Glacial Journeys of the Heart

As I open the vault, a frosty breeze flies,
With mysteries wrapped in old foil and lies.
A frozen bouquet of sad, wilted greens,
Reminds me of love's many, varied scenes.

My heart on ice, with plenty to explore,
Each veggie a chapter, and so much more.
From leafy romaine to a rogue garlic clove,
This haphazard trip tells me where I rove.

Frost covered fish lay in wait for a friend,
Their watery whispers beg me to blend.
Yet here in the chill, I find solace and cheer,
In the quirkiest moments, the heart dares to steer.

An icy escape from the usual grind,
With laughter and jokes tucked away in my mind.
In this glacial journey, I'll celebrate me,
In frost and in humor, I set my heart free.

Visions of Ice and Thought

In the cool of the freezer, my thoughts start to swirl,
A frosty direction, an ice-cream-filled whirl.
With pints of reflection, I ponder and muse,
What meals I've neglected, what joys I refuse.

Mushy peas linger, their green smiles so bright,
While frozen lasagna waves warm with delight.
In the chill of the night, I dance through my head,
Finding new reasons to not go to bed.

Ice cubes like glitter, they shimmer and clang,
Echoing laughter from old parties, they sang.
Each frosted morsel, a story to unfold,
In this icy retreat, I'm ever so bold.

So here's to the laughter hidden in frost,
In the icy abyss, nothing here feels lost.
With humor and heart, I've realized today,
Even cold can be cozy; it's all in the play.

The Chill of Unfulfilled Hopes

In my fridge, dreams sit tight,
Frozen in a frosty flight.
I open the door, they all sneak,
Whispering thoughts that feel so bleak.

Lettuce lays in leafy shame,
While my ambitions play a game.
Ice cubes clink, they laugh at me,
Chillin' while I ponder glee.

Beneath the Ice, the Fire Rages

Behind the frosty, glassy veil,
Passion's warmth begins to pale.
A pizza slice dreams of its rise,
Yet survives in chilly disguise.

Hot sauce waits for its embrace,
Trapped in a congealed space.
The banquet of dreams sits in frost,
Yet hunger's fire cannot be lost.

Querying the Frosted Layers of Reality

I peer through the white, thick frost,
Seeking truths that seem long lost.
Frosted veggies, shining bright,
Hide the wonders out of sight.

I ask the peas, do you know why,
We freeze our dreams and let them lie?
They giggle softly, oh so sly,
Saying, 'Just wait, we'll tell you why!'

A Glimpse into the Frozen Abyss

In the depths of the chilly chest,
I see regrets, I see the best.
A yogurt cup, a sorbet thrill,
Wondering if they'll ever chill.

With frosty smiles, they beckon me,
To unravel what it's meant to be.
But all I find is cold despair,
A frosted maze, and empty air.

The Cool Comfort of Solitude

In the chilly depths, I find my peace,
Frosted thoughts that never cease.
Ice cubes dance in cups so bright,
A frozen world feels just right.

Leftovers whisper tales of yore,
Quiet echoes of meals before.
In solitude, with snacks I thrive,
Frozen veggies keep hope alive.

Unthawing Heartbeats of Tomorrow

Wait for the melt, the ticking time,
Where icy dreams begin to climb.
Tomorrow's thaw brings warmth and cheer,
But first, I munch on treats right here.

With every beep, the microwave sings,
Love's a dance of frozen flings.
Popcorn kernels leap for joy,
Unthawing hearts, life's silly ploy.

Frigid Puzzles of Existence

In the frosty void, I ponder well,
Is that ice cream a secret spell?
Frigid barriers, cold as stone,
But solve the puzzle, I'm not alone.

Each frosty bite holds wisdom sweet,
Pantry secrets, a brain freeze treat.
Beyond the frost, a truth can gleam,
That frozen stuff is part of the dream.

Chilling Tales of the Unfrozen

Once there lived a brave old pie,
In the freezer, it learned to fly.
Chilling tales of desserts untold,
Dreams of warmth, daring and bold.

A frosty world, a frozen friend,
With jokes and gags that just won't end.
Out of the cold, the laughter springs,
Life's wacky dance of freeze-frame things.

Icy Chronicles of Hidden Joys

In the fridge where laughter stays,
Old leftovers join the craze.
A pizza slice, a single wing,
Telling tales of every fling.

Chilly friends from yesteryears,
Cold confessions mixed with beers.
Each frosty bite brings back the cheer,
Whispers echo, 'We were here!'

Broccoli shivers with delight,
As ice cubes dance in the night.
A treasure trove of joy and fun,
In the freezer, laughs are spun.

So here's to all the frosty finds,
With silly names and silly minds.
In the cold, we can reflect,
On fun times we won't forget.

The Stillness Between Two Beats

Time stands still in a frosty nook,
Waiting lips that love to cook.
Half-eaten cakes, a secret stash,
Frozen dreams in a happy clash.

Heartbeat pauses by the ice,
As I savor something nice.
A popsicle of memories sweet,
Tasting life's little, chilly feat.

The stillness shakes with laughter's cheer,
While ice cream sings, 'I'll be here!'
A moment caught, a little freeze,
In this silence, hearts find ease.

So grab a spoon and dig away,
In the cold, we find our play.
Each frozen bite a giggle, too,
The world may wait, but we know the view.

Frosted Lullabies of Remembered Love

In a box where memories chill,
Frozen kisses, what a thrill!
Chocolate fudge and cherry pie,
Whispered secrets, oh my, oh my!

Each frosty bite recalls the spark,
Of candlelit nights and laughter's mark.
Eager berries dive in sweet,
Melodies find their frosty beat.

A scoop of joy, a dollop of fun,
With every bite, the past is spun.
In icy depths, these tales remain,
Frosted love that won't be slain.

So toast with spoons, let laughter flow,
In this chilly world, love's the glow.
Frozen memories we still adore,
In the sweetness, we find more.

A Vault of Frozen Memories

In this vault of chilly keeps,
Every bite a memory leaps.
Mashed potatoes in a line,
Whisper stories, oh so fine.

Ice cream dreams and cake galore,
Remind us of what we adore.
Chilled delights that never fade,
In this vault, our laughter's laid.

A frosty landscape, smiles abound,
In the freezer, joys are found.
Pickles dressed in frosty wear,
Update old tales with a flair.

So open wide that freezer door,
Let memories spill out and soar.
For in these frozen treasures, you'll see,
A vault of joy, forever free.

Chilled Certainties of the Heart

In the cold, I keep my fears,
Wrapped in ice, like forgotten tears.
Frosty joy, with a wink so sly,
A frozen laugh that dares to fly.

Pickles dance in their glass jar,
Relishing dreams from near and far.
Ice cream scoops with whimsical glee,
Chilling hopes that set me free.

I find solace in chilly bites,
Sipping soup beneath soft lights.
Each spoonful a warm embrace,
While frosty winds pick up the pace.

So here I stand, a cool delight,
In my freezer, all feels right.
Laughter mingles with the frost,
In this chill, I find what's lost.

The Icy Lens of Experience

Through the glass of my icy view,
I see the world in shades of blue.
Frozen thoughts swirl like a dance,
A frosty whimsy, a silly chance.

On a whim, I toss in some peas,
Shouting, 'Chill out!' to the summer breeze.
Reality melts beneath my scoop,
As I sip on laughs, a frosty soup.

Each beam of light, a spark of fun,
Crisp winter nights, where giggles run.
Life's a laugh when served in freeze,
Cracked humor like ice on the knees.

So I peer through my icy glare,
Finding joy in the subzero air.
zI chuckle at what melts away,
The ridiculousness keeps blues at bay.

Frigid Dreams in a Warm World

In the freezer, where dreams reside,
I stash my worries, take them for a ride.
Ice cubes jingle, a merry sound,
In frosty realms, pure joy is found.

Popcorn kernels, they freeze with pride,
Frigid secrets they cannot hide.
I hear their whispers, soft and sweet,
As they freeze, they trip on their feet.

Beneath the ice cream, hopes do float,
With frosty sprinkles, I take note.
Chilling stories baked in frost,
The warmth outside, a happy cost.

So let the winter come alive,
With frozen dreams that thrill and strive.
In this jolly icy embrace,
I find my place, my merry space.

Crystalized Thoughts in the Quiet Night

Under starry skies, the coolness spreads,
Creativity blooms inside my head.
Thoughts crystallize like frosted panes,
Reflecting laughter, clearing stains.

A midnight snack, a secret delight,
Dancing like stars in the inky night.
Frosted cupcakes, a sweet surprise,
With a wink and a nod, they rise.

In whispers, the ice makes its case,
With each crisp bite, I find my grace.
Laughter echoes, a frosty tune,
Under the gaze of a playful moon.

So here I sit, in frozen thought,
With each chilly giggle that I've caught.
A night with whimsy, a clear delight,
In the freeze of joy, everything's right.

The Frosted Path of the Forgotten

In the back of the icebox, dreams lie so still,
Chilling in silence, with time they will thrill.
A frozen pizza waits for a long-lost night,
While ice cream whispers of sweet, frosty light.

Old leftovers grumble of dinners past gone,
Each wrapped in mystery, like an old, tired song.
They beckon with laughter, so frozen and bright,
In their icy embrace, the world feels just right.

Hopes Stored Side by Side

In the frosty abyss, hopes collide with a laugh,
Containers of dreams, neatly packed like a craft.
With peas filled with wisdom, and corn full of cheer,
Each bite holds the promise, of what will appear.

The grapes, frozen with time, dance in jolly delight,
While forgotten fries whisper, 'Hey, we're alright!'
Side by side, they gather, each one tells a tale,
In a symphony chilly, a frosty detail.

The Cool Embrace of Forgotten Dreams

Behind frosted glass, hopes twirl in a freeze,
Meeting each other with a mischievous tease.
There's a sandwich from sorrows, a pie made of thrill,
Their laughter resounds like a sweet, icy chill.

A cake with a candle, long past its due date,
Stands proud in the corner, saying, 'Isn't it fate?'
In this cool embrace, dreams are safe to explore,
Like treasures stored neatly in a frosty décor.

Whispering Frost in the Silence

In the quiet of night, when the world is asleep,
The frost starts to shimmer, its secrets to keep.
Containers of laughter, wrapped in their shells,
Share stories of fun, in the coolness they dwell.

Muffins once plump now giggle with glee,
While the ice cubes rattle, oh what could they be?
Each frozen delight, a chuckle in freeze,
In the kitchen's cold heart, humor flows with ease.

Congealed Thoughts of the Soul

In the depths of the cold, I ponder my fate,
The ice cubes are laughing, it's never too late.
My dreams are like popsicles, frozen and bright,
I scoop them on Sundays, to savor the bite.

The fridge hums a tune, a jolly old song,
Where leftovers linger, and pickles belong.
I search through the shelves for a hint of delight,
A half-eaten cupcake, all frosted and white.

Chasing my thoughts through the bottles and jars,
The mustard a witness to all of my scars.
Each frosty encounter, a memory stuck,
While veggies in Tupperware can't bring me luck.

A reflection of life in this chilly domain,
I laugh at the moments, I dance in the brain.
Perhaps in the ice, I'll find truths tucked away,
In the doodles of grocery lists meant to decay.

Frosty Encounters with the Self

I opened the freezer, a world of surprises,
Where frozen-bag dreams are the greatest disguises.
With each icy door swing, I laugh and I reel,
At dinners I prepped, that now seem surreal.

A fortress of flavors in half-empty tubs,
Craving some laughter, I binge on the jugs.
The frozen peas wink, they know all my thoughts,
While ribs in the back are the ghosts that I fought.

In the chill, there's comfort, in flavors I trust,
As my self-reflection develops a crust.
The popsicles giggle, they chime with my glee,
They tell me I'm great because I'm frosty free!

So I lift a frosty drink, and toast to the gloom,
Where ice hides the secrets, but joy fills the room.
Through sugar and salt, my heart learns to cheer,
In the frost, I find laughter, and that's what's most dear.

A Portrait in Ice

Here lies a portrait, but what's in the frame?
A jigsaw of vegetables, each one has a name.
Carrots in jackets, the broccoli bright,
Together they shimmer in the soft, cool light.

I marvel the icebergs, stacked high in the box,
Wonders of freezing, like whimsical clocks.
The humor of time, all twirled up and spry,
With a smile from spinach that makes me deny.

As I rummage through treasures, some ancient, some new

I fuse all the flavors, it's a wild rendezvous!
The laughter of leftovers, a playful ballet,
While frozen fruit giggles, they dance and sway.

What's frozen may melt, but the joy won't defrost,
As I savor my moments, with nothing to cost.
In coldness I wander, with whimsy as my guide,
Finding treasures of laughter in the chill, and with pride.

Numbing Revelations

The freezer is lurking, it holds many tales,
Of meals that I planned and snacks that turned pale.
From toast crumbs to muffin caps, laughter ignites,
With each frosted reveal, my sanity fights.

I dump out the ice cream, my purest delight,
Spoon in one hand, in the other, my plight.
The fudge ripple waves remind me to chill,
As I ponder existence while raiding the grill.

Here, thoughts become numbing, like endless cold packs,
I sit with my sorrows, the kitchen, no lack.
As I munch on a burrito, a strange quest unfolds,
To savor the moments while the ice slowly holds.

Each bite brings me wisdom, each crunch a new scheme,
In this frostbitten realm, where absurdity beams.
So I scoop out my laughter, from depths oh so bold,
In the frosty reflections, my stories are told.

The Fridge of Forgotten Aspirations

In the fridge, dreams chill away,
Forgotten hopes in yesterday's tray.
A half-eaten pizza, a star's wane,
Who knew success came with sour grain?

Leftovers of plans, all wrapped in foil,
Each one a memory, a past to uncoil.
Dare I dig deep and find a lost goal?
Or just stick to snacks, that's easier, whole!

What Lies Beneath the Polar Surface

Beneath frost and ice, some secrets hide,
Like unturned veggies on a frosty ride.
A journey of snacks that never took flight,
What stories they tell in the pale moonlight!

The iceberg lettuce, with dreams so grand,
Once vibrant and fresh, now a wilted band.
A laugh from the coleslaw, slawing away,
Chasing bright visions that went astray!

Slices of Time

Each slice of cake a memory's cheer,
In the layers of time, some taste bitter fear.
Frosting of laughter, nuts of delight,
Did I bake it right or leave it too tight?

The clock ticks on; is that cheesecake past?
A slice of ambition, thick and steadfast.
With every bite, oh what tales unfold,
Some sweet triumphs and some tales of old.

Shelved and Frozen

On the shelves of dreams, items stack high,
Frozen ambitions like pizza pie.
I ponder the thrill of that muffin tin,
What spurs me to bake? Where do I begin?

Resolutions cling like cling wrap so tight,
Years in the freezer, just out of sight.
Each container tells of a goal on the run,
Yet here I remain, too comfy to stun!

The Mind's Cold Storage

In the brain's freezer, ideas lie still,
Chilling with thoughts; oh what a thrill!
An avalanche of why's, a blizzard of who,
Glimpsing the dreams that once sparkled like dew.

I sift through the frosty, tomes of the past,
Each nugget of wisdom, forever amassed.
But here in this cold, with laughs mixed with dread,
I'll thaw out my dreams with a warm piece of bread!

www.ingramcontent.com/pod-product-compliance
Lightning Source LLC
Chambersburg PA
CBHW051637160426
43209CB00004B/690